Special Dedication

This book is inspired by the immeasurable love I have for my amazing son, Justin. What a privilege and honor it is to be his mother and greatest fan through each chapter of his life! We have developed an unshakable bond that I will eternally treasure. He is now an adult, yet he will forever be my baby, sun, moon, stars, and truly the most wonderful blessing in my life. I love you more than a million stars.

A special thank you to beautiful Carmen, for introducing me to the Canva Platform.

From the moment they are born, it is crucial that, as parents, we let our children know, through both words and actions, that they are needed, appreciated, and loved unconditionally. Let us be available to them and truly delighted to be in their presence, so they feel seen, heard, understood, and accepted. Being a mom is such an honor and the most beautiful joy on earth. As parents, we experience the greatest and deepest of all loves. I hope this book captivates both your and your child's hearts for years to come. It is an absolute joy to be able to share such love, fun, and encouragement with you. May the messages of love and beautiful illustrations fill your heart with all the smiles, wonder, and joy they bring to me.

Let us thank God for allowing us to share in a love closest to His agape love for us.

Thank you CANVA, for providing the beautiful art illustrations that make it possible to create these wonderful, colorful, and exciting stories of hope and love.

This Book Belongs To:

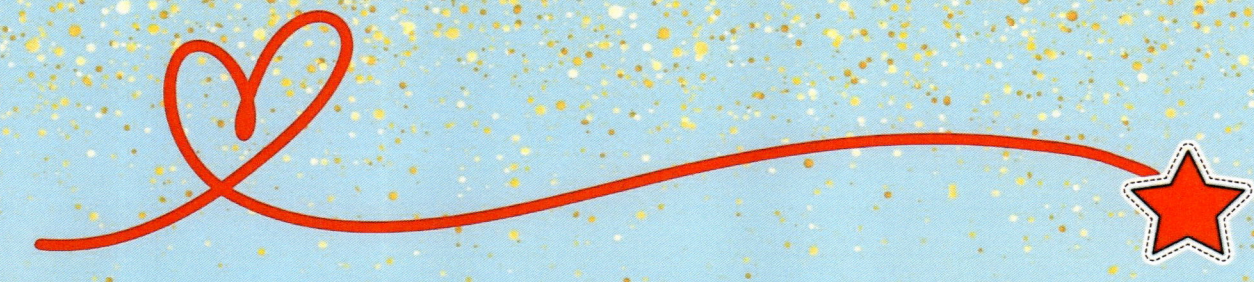

i love you

IT'S A GIRL

IT'S A BOY

When you were born,

What a *wonderful* day.

For you to be *healthy*,

I always would *pray*.

I ♥ YOU

When I saw your sweet face, it was then that I knew.

The joy of my heart is being with you.

When *I wake up* in the morning,
And *sleep* at nighttime, too,
Each and every single day,
You turn my *gray* skies *blue*.

You are my *precious* and *beautiful* treasure.

My *love* for you *grows* beyond **measure**.

When you wake up feeling *happy*, even when you're feeling *sad*,
I'm *delighted* you belong to me; this makes my heart so *glad*.

MONDAY TUESDAY WEDNESDAY THURSDAY
FRIDAY SATURDAY SUNDAY

Each day of the week,

from *morning* until *night*,

I'm *excited* for all we'll see and do.

You are my *shining light*.

I LOVE YOU

Some days, I'll see you *smile*.

Other times, I'll see you *frown*.

I'm *happy* to be by your side,

Whether you're *up* or *down*.

As you *grow* and *learn*, with every passing day,

I will be here to *support* you, in every single way.

However you are feeling is *okay*.

I'm *with you* every step of the way.

Whatever you are *feeling*,

Even when you are *afraid*,

I'll be here *now* and *always*,

My *love* will never fade.

I'm *happy* and *delighted*

to hear all about your *day*.

We'll *talk* it through *together*.

I'll *listen* to all you have to *say*.

you
and
me

So many *fun* things...how will I *choose*?

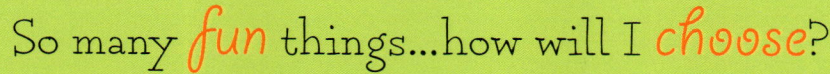

do your best

keep at it

You might *change* your mind

with each passing day.

This is part of *growing* up

and perfectly *okay*.

When you have a *question*
or just don't understand,
it's *okay* to *ask* for *help*.
So, be *brave* and raise your hand.

YOU CAN

YOU GOT THIS

I am so *grateful* for you.

The *adventures* we'll have will be so much *fun*.

A lifetime of *smiles* that has just begun.

I *love* being with you and *enjoying* our time.

I want you to know, I'm so *thankful* you're mine.

When others are mean or don't want to *share*,
be *proud* to be you and show *loving* care.
Make the *best choice* and do what is *right*,
Let *kindness* shine like a *twinkling* light.

I'm so *excited*
for our trip to the zoo.
Oh, how I have waited
to *share* this with you.

We'll see all the *animals*, one by one.
Your *face* warms my *heart*
like the *dazzling* sun.

Summertime will be so very *fun*.

Laughing and *playing* in the sun.

Sand **squishy** so **squashy** between our toes.

My *love* for you just *grows* and *grows*.

Springtime flowers are in *bloom*,

Your *giggles* bring me *cheer*.

The bees are busy *buzzing* and making honey,

What a *wonderful* time of year.

SPRING

Let It Snow

So much *fun* in the winter *snow*,
You are so *important* to me.
I will *help* you build a *snowman*,
How truly *amazing* this will be.

In the winter,

as the *rain* falls down,

this may turn your *smile*

into a frown.

As the rain stops, you can *splash* in that puddle,

a colorful *rainbow* appears as we sit and *cuddle*.

Autumn leaves falling down, What *beautiful* colors you'll see.

Tossing them *high* in the *sky*, As they glide down from the tree.

Dry and *crackly* under your feet, They'll go *crunch* with your shoe.

So much *laughter* there will be, As *I share* this day with you.

Storytime for *nighty night*,
We'll always be a *team*.
Soon those *sleepy* eyes will close,
As you fall asleep and *dream*.

See all the cute *duckies* in a pond.
As they follow their *mommy*,
Right where they *belong*.

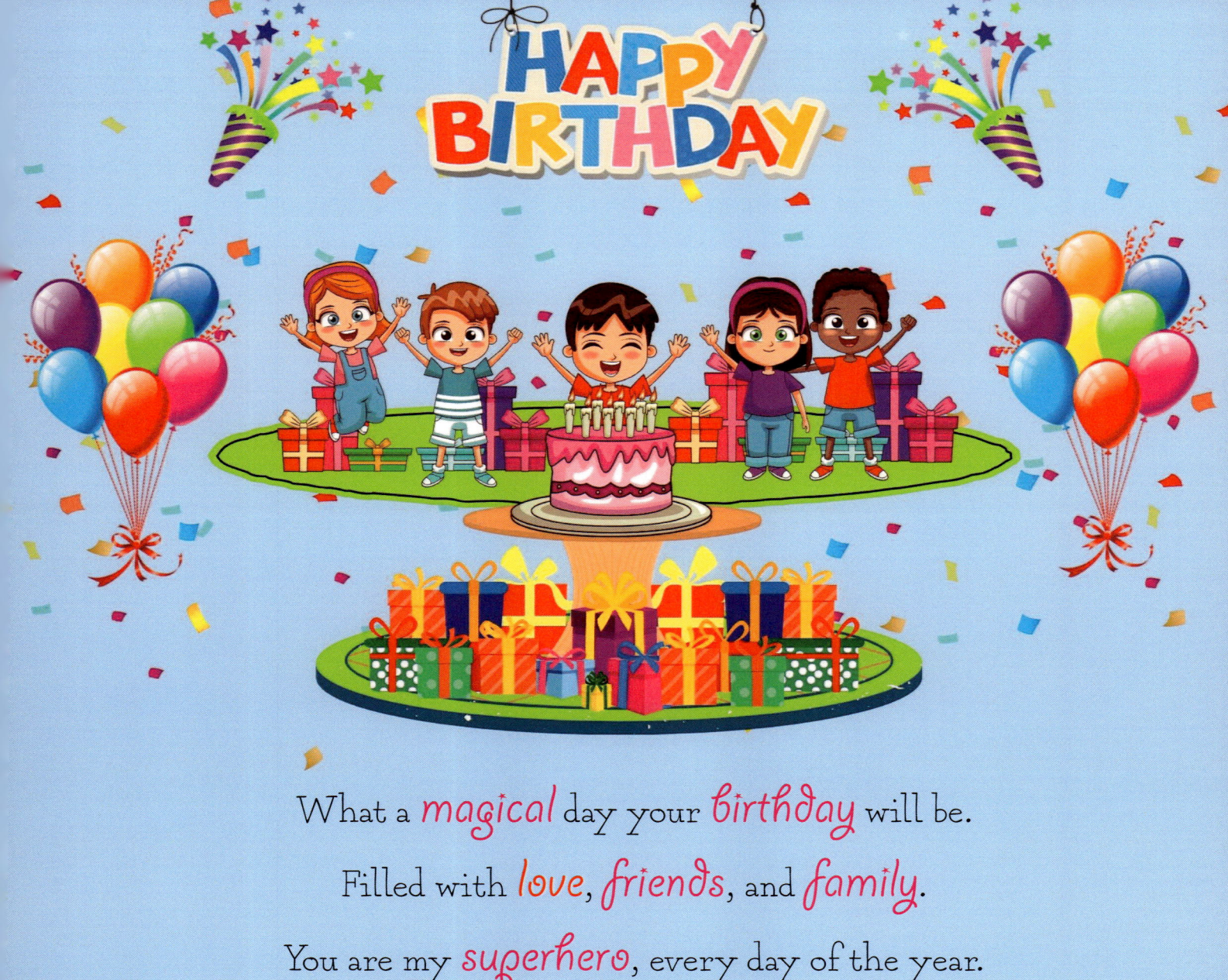

What a *magical* day your *birthday* will be.

Filled with *love*, *friends*, and *family*.

You are my *superhero*, every day of the year.

Let's sing *Happy Birthday*,

With *laughter* and *cheer*.

Now it's time for your ABCs.

You'll also *learn* to count to three.

One day you'll even count to ten.

And be *happy* to start all over again.

I'm so very *delighted, joyful,* and *proud.*

Let's stand up and *cheerfully,*

Sing out loud.

COOL

AMAZING

Your *favorite* place, we can go. Where could this possibly be?

Wherever we are, we'll have lots of *fun*, with *love* and *family*.

I'm so *excited* to *bake* with you.

Cakes, Cupcakes and Cookies too.

How *tasty* they'll be inside our *tummies*.

Made with such *love* and oh so *yummy*.

For all of my life, I've *waited* for *you*.

To know you are mine, is a *dream* come true.

For all of my life, you're the *joy* of my *heart*.

I've *loved* you so *dearly*, from the very start.

My *love* is a *circle*, To which there is *no end*.

You are my *precious* child, And my very *best friend*.

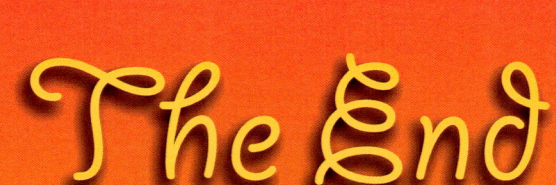

The End